SIZE MATTERS!

HOW BIG IS YOUR SOCIAL FOOTPRINT?

ALEX PUTMAN

ISBN **978-0-9893835-0-9**

In loving memory of my late "Granny" who was my mother, grandmother and spiritual guide. I believe you can see the fruits of your labor. Thank you for teaching me, see you again someday.

Contents

BE YOURSELF

INNOVATE

GET SOCIAL

Acknowledgments

I owe a debt of gratitude to many people in achieving the life-long dream of publishing my first book.

Thank you to my life mate, wife and babies momma, Tifany, for her authentic critiques, long standing friendship and unwavering support. You have always believed in my potential and supported most of my big ideas. No truer words have been spoken than those read at our wedding.

Love suffers long and is kind; love does not envy; love does not parade itself, is not puffed up; does not behave rudely, does not seek its own, is not provoked, thinks no evil; does not rejoice in iniquity, but rejoices in the truth; bears all things, believes all things, hopes all things, endures all things. Love never fails.

Huge thanks to my children, Alexis, Kathryn, Gabrielle and Corban. This book is possible because your eight little eyes provide me with a new world view. Remember *"I love you more today than yesterday and will love you more than that tomorrow"!* Your creativity has allowed me to tap into my inner child and see the world differently.

At 8 years old, our household television died. During this "tragedy" I was "forced" to read books. Reading the classics as a youth took me to places where my pocketbook never could. Thanks to everyone that ever gave me a book (and underwear) for Christmas!

Special thanks to members of my creative team for their dedication and assistance during the writing process. Anastasia Bartolucci, one of my best hires, gives hope to her generation. Thank you for your creative genius and being the more like a younger sister. Thanks to Sandy Yun for your creative designs on the book covers. Your considerable patience and kind heart made this an easy and beautiful process. Thanks Sarah Aubin-Barrett for your funky web designs and ability to create a story through web pages.

Thanks Brian Cunningham for keeping it real at all times. Your life is a testimony to good living. Thank for your support, wisdom and foresight. You are a true brother and the only guy outside of a blood relative that I can comfortable say "love you man"!

Special thanks to my Aunts Margarette, Nadra and Lucy for their guidance and inspiration during my youth and my dad who was a single father of two rambunctious boys.

Lastly, there are three things that get me through this life; Faith, Family and Fun! These three life views have delivered me through many a rough patch; without this life would be pointless.

Why Size Matters!

I have been in talent acquisition and human resources since 1996, assisting and watching many companies grow rapidly in short spurts. This has been a consistent joy and opportunity to be part of someone's career growth and progression. In all the years the one distinguisher, the separator of talent at any level has been the ability to properly market or brand one's self as the best for the role.

Over the past decade, a major shift has occurred: the marketing of self. In the past you were entrenched in an organization or company where results were measured, hard work was recognized by upper management and the "team player" was the last person to leave. Careers blossomed over drinks and management made decisions as a result of word-of-mouth marketing.

In today's work climate this has all changed. Companies need to grow rapidly and will go on hiring binges, ramping up for the next big project and expand their talent pool without thought to budgets only to later implode due to a lack of proper forecasting. Talented employees are released due to these "cutbacks" or "unforeseen market changes", all of which is completely out of the control of the employee.

So what can employees control? How do you protect your career from the corporate saboteur who provides little thought into the derailment of your career path? Personal Branding!

People often think of branding as a marketing term referring to a product or tangible item. Enter the social age; an age where your actions, location updates and acts of indiscretion are captured and stored for the world to see. Twenty year veterans scoff at the idea of social media playing a role in their career, but think about this, why do companies spend millions of dollars to run a commercial during the Super Bowl? It's not only to sell more products, it is also to gain support for the company from investors, reassure board members and remind people that they are relevant, BIG or just GREAT!

What if Nike never ran another commercial for Air Jordan's? Eventually the only people wearing them would be sixty year old men who "remember when"...... You need people to "remember now".... think of every social update, every tweet, and every video/picture upload as a personal webmercial marketing YOU!

This book will take you through the role of social media as a self-branding tool used to grow and develop your career. You will walk away with the ability to build a strong digital presence utilizing many of the strategies and social platforms available today. You will also gain key insider knowledge of my years of interviewing experience where you will learn what employers are seeking and their interviewing techniques.

So regardless of your current career position; entry level, newbie, experienced or jobseeker, this book will assist in building a personal brand that is BIG, because **size does matter!**

10 Commandments of Social Media

Thousands of years ago, people were given a set of 10 commandments which were a set of simple guidelines covering every ethical or morale question with a simplistic answer. During the first few hundred years of their existence, people created add-on rules (600+) that took away from their simplicity.

One of my main goals in writing this book is to simplify social media code and provide people with an easy format to control their careers with 10 simple commandments of social media:

1.	Be careful how you spend your social time, too much of something becomes your focus and takes your eyes off what really matters.
2.	Don't use OMG as a negative; he didn't make you do anything.
3.	Get your nose out of your screens; 24/7 365 of anything is dangerous. Take a break at least one day per week.
4.	Connect to your parents. Remember they gave you life and most likely support you in other ways; thank them!
5.	Fear leads to anger, anger leads to hate, hate leads to suffering and suffering leads to darkness; don't fear anything!
6.	Liars suck, don't suck!
7.	Killing is more than a physical action; don't kill off the joys of life or your dreams by not putting yourself out there!
8.	Don't steal content! Recreate, rebrand and reimagine!
9.	Cheaters never win and cheaters take shortcuts! Work at it every day and whatever it is will pay off!

10. Don't be jealous of the success of others nor take pride in their down times! Kick some butt yourself and always be happy for the success of others. Amen.

It is very easy to get caught up in the world of social media - like crack it can be addictive and lead one to a zombie-like state of disillusion. Crack-heads did not wake up one day and decide to be addicts, and no one starts out in social media to harm others. Along the way they fail to follow the simplest of rules, the Golden Rule "***do unto others***"....use it to help grow your brand and the brand of others. Be an open networker and let's all work together to achieve the goals of a large footprint!

Chapter 1

What is a Personal Brand?

"Content is King" – Bill Gates

The dictionary defines a brand as: kind, grade, or make, as indicated by a stamp, trademark, or the like: the best brand of coffee OR a mark made by burning or otherwise, to indicate kind, grade, make, ownership, etc....

A brand is created, built and nurtured; it evokes a personal connection or desire to the end user. Brands have a personality; they create a desire among the senses and stand for a belief or something larger than just a logo or image. Your goal is to create this same emotion when people observe your personal brand!

In 2006, after going through a shutdown with a major company and working for a short stint in an industry I had no passion for, I decided it was time to take matters into my own hands. My exact sentiment was "I will never rely on a company for my career progression and professional success!" On that day, I began a crusade to become the most networked person in the Atlanta, Georgia area, believing it's all about who you know! I incorporated and began working on logo designs to separate my corporation and set myself apart! I wanted that Nike swoosh or the silver apple that people would look at and know this is the man! Later the realization hit me; I was focused on the wrong things...I made it about a logo, not about the contents of the company; I did not make it personal!

Brands are not simply a logo or image. Many people make the mistake of thinking that creating multiple profiles across the social media landscape will suffice and land them their dream job because someone found their mark interesting. A logo or image does not evoke a connection until well after the brand is established. You are early in your brand, so a logo will not suffice.

In the early 90's there was a musical genius named Prince. He is an icon on pop culture, but decided to change his name to a symbol and referred to himself as "the artist formerly known as Prince". He is by all measures equal in popularity to The Beatles, Michael Jackson, Jay Z or any other artist you can imagine.

You are not him, so don't try to logo yourself! Show his symbol to one of your professors or a parent and ask them what it stands for…most likely they will not know, but ask them if they recall the musical pop icon Prince and they will!

Ask yourself these questions:

- What do I want to represent?
- What do I believe in and stand for?
- What are my values and things that absolutely will not change?

Your brand must reflect the answers to these questions and this will not be captured simply in a logo or design. It takes years for people to truly know who they are and have real answers to these questions. Once you know the answers to "who am I" you are ready to market yourself to the twitterverse / new media world; a world of short messages aimed at an Attention Deficit Disorderly world.

Early in my career, as a Southern transplant to Ohio, I was responsible for recruiting people by cold calling into organizations and getting the names of their employees. The goal was to attract their employees from their current jobs and place at my client for a large fee. One of the common methods implored by several teammates was a ruse. See, if you called the front desk and asked for "the mechanical engineer" you were met with a "what is this in regards to?" You cannot respond "I am a recruiter, hoping to pluck your employee away and place them at another company for a huge fee". So, many people would lie and say "I am a college student, writing a term paper and hoping to gather information about your business".

This went against my innate belief and desire not to lie. Should I not have taken the job? Was I required to utilize this method? No, the ruse was an option, however there were several options. Lying was one option but becoming more creative was another. Instead of the ruse approach I developed the "southern sweetness approach", where I would call in and conduct the following call;

> **Me**: *"Hello this is Alex, may I speak with John in engineering" (deep southern twang)*
>
> **Unknown Cold Call Response**, *"we don't have a John"*
>
> **Me:** *"Oh, well who is the mechanical engineer there?"*
>
> **Irritated unknown cold call response** *" what is this in regards to"*
>
> **Me:** *" I am a junior recruiter and attempting to get in touch with someone from your engineering department"*

Surprised I told the truth Response: *"ok, perhaps you need to speak with Frank"....* **OR many times** *"we don't take those calls....."*

I would then strike up a conversation with the reception area and ask about their day! How they liked working for XYZ Company. I am naturally an extrovert, an honest, nice guy who enjoys speaking with people. My honesty did not always pay off but many times it did. Just as the ruse of "I am a college student writing a paper" did not pay off, because when the person got on the phone and was told a student was calling them and then realized it was a lie, the trust was already broken.

Build YOUR brand, not someone else's!!

Your Brand Starts NOW!

I have a friend that lived the rock n roll dream. He was a drum major at a nationally recognized university and after school lived the lifestyle, playing in a popular underground band and building a legendary following all before the age of 22! In an effort to remind him that he never wanted to work for "the man", he selected a wide array of body art to ensure he would stick to his word, he tattooed his arms and chest in every visible spot. Fast forward to the age of 28, he is finishing a degree in finance and the 1st round of tattoo removal treatments.

Your social footprint or brand image is no different! Students starting out are at the age of underage drinking; partying till the early morning hours and allowing social access to every person you party with any given night. Do you believe they have your best social footprint in mind? Have you plead guilty to PUI (posting under the influence) and wished you could take it back (and deleting it does not count)! But let's not stop there.....how about video reminders of these events posted to your YouTube channel and viewed by 18 of your closest friends!

I once hired a young man who was a referral from an employee and close friend. Shortly after beginning employment, his friends tip us off about a YouTube channel where the employee would post drunken rants! In all honesty, it was entertaining. How do you think his manager felt about an employee posting drunken rants? What do most people rant about? Work! Granted the videos had less than 35 views, but the point is that his brand is out there for anyone to find! GooeyPooeyBear should have read a book about his personal brand!

Much like the tattoos, the day will come when you decide that perhaps those PUI's were not worth it and that maybe, just maybe, you should have been more careful. That day typically rears its head in your quest for a job or career move! Before you begin the pursuit of mass branding, consider a few little things that will matter at some point down the road.

Screen Names

Most people never think about the simple task of selecting a name for their social channels. You may go with the randomly assigned name which adds zero brand value. Chances are your name is already taken and "JohnSmith6795" does not appeal to you. You decide that why not be funny and use something unique like, "sleepwheniamdead69". Fast-forward several videos, thousands of pictures and many new platforms later. "Sleepwheniamdead69" is a distant memory, you have matured and decided that "bigdaddylovehandles" better suits the more mature you!

Time marches on and enough people have mentioned your user name and you have received many blank looks from the human resource associate emailing your personal account that you realize in all your wisdom, "johnsmith6795" does not seem so bad. The footprints are still left and a quick search reveals that "sleepwheniamdead69", "bigdaddylovehandles" and "johnsmith6795" are all the same person and you were actually on MySpace and friends with the ever classy "Mercedes68andoweyou1".

Footprints on the Screen

Your future, potential employers will scrub the internet in search of who you are, not only employers but the background companies they utilize. This is not a threat! I do it every day and speak with background companies that offer "social network scrubbing" as a buying advantage! Some employers will understand that you were just being foolish but others may not be so forgiving in their narrow mind of doubt, thus going with "Goodie2Shoes" because he/she came up clean with no "red flags". Is it legal to judge an employee by their social footprint? Yes and no (depends on what you find). In the scenarios above, this would not be legal….but how will you know this is the reason?

Currently there are background services that will scrub all social profiles for employers for each potential hire for the cost of a decent meal. These services are looking for and will find any knuckleheaded, derogatory or inflammatory comments you have ever posted. In your Pabst Blue Ribbon or Jack Daniels state of mind that may have been forgotten. Next thing you

know "sleepwheniamdead69" is
"sleepinmomanddadsbasementtiliamdead" because you are
unable to find a job!

**Do you and your parent's basement a favor; PROTECT YOUR
BRAND!**

Google Yourself Regularly

Once I was presenting to a group of college students in a large
lecture hall on how to find a job utilizing social media. I proudly
announced that they should all "Google themselves". As the
roar of laughter filled the hall, I realized how "dirty" this could
sound. But you should really Google yourself regularly, doing it
by yourself will prevent lots of issues ☺.

I was discussing Google alerts (http://www.google.com/alerts)
with someone regarding her college age daughter who had an
underage drinking infraction. Now this may not seem a HUGE
deal as it happens on a regular basis and most employers chalk
it up as a "kid mistake". This particular young lady was involved
in the world of pageantry and, of course, those ladies are
expected to represent a higher standard.

When you Google her name, guess what appears on page one?
Yep, her underage drinking arrest that was posted in the school
newspaper! At some point her mug shot may appear as there
are groups (http://www.mugshotsonline.com) that put these up
just so you have to pay to take them down! The mom did not
realize it would rank so high in Google search, her question:
"How do you get rid of this?" You really are unable to, unless
you have a few pages worth of material that ranks higher than
the sites hosting these stories and pictures. Her mom's

response, "Crap, this is the first thing that any potential employer is going to see!"

There are worse things than "googling" yourself (insert 6th grade humor)! It may cause shock, irritation or self-realization, but will not cause blindness.

Components of a Brand

It seems that everybody wants to be a reality star, and given the field of competition, it may not be a difficult challenge. But why? Why is it that a group of lackluster talent (unless you include speaking in an unintelligible garble with script rolling at the bottom of the screen "talent") can get drunk, naked and downright stupid, yet people want more? Why does our society create the reality "stars" and give them so much hope for fame and fortune?

It's because as untalented and uncouth as they may be, the reality star makes a connection. This is why every show has a villain, good guy, sweet girl, someone with an alternate lifestyle choice, family person etc.... It's why boy bands have existed since the 60's with The Beatles, The Monkey's, New Edition, New Kids on the Block, Backstreet Boys, NSync and One Direction, there is someone for everyone to love and hate!

Brands typically work the same way. They evoke an internal feeling that arouses something within the consumer. Even if you are not trying to build a personal brand, your brand exists. Even if a company never airs the first commercial, the company still exists and has a reputation and invokes some type of response at the mention of their name. Understanding the invocation of feelings will help in designing the strategies for your brand!

The five categories include:

1. Emotion
2. Beliefs
3. Desires
4. Senses
5. Personality

Emotion

One of the reasons social media has grown is due to the emotional connections it provides. It allows us to stay connected with friends, family, actors, actresses, athletes, musicians and even world leaders! Never before has the world been so connected with accessibility to megastars! We can engage them in conversation and become a part of their world. And this feels great; it makes us feel part of something bigger.

The same holds true for a company. I know people that hate their jobs, however will never leave because they love the people they work with! We all want to feel part of something; it's just that now you can really see inside an organization even from your mobile device! Some companies do a great job of portraying the perfect world (beware of this lie) yet others don't tell enough. You now have an access that was not available to people in 2005 or earlier. You can connect at almost the highest level of an organization with the click of a mouse and feel part of the organization even before you apply for the job.

What emotion are you invoking when people review your social networks? Extended tenure with an organization may evoke the emotional reaction "must be a hard worker". Lots of jobs in short periods of time may evoke a fear of disloyalty? Seeing title changes in increments at the same company evoke career advancement so must be excellent at their job?

Understand that your social footprint will create an image that stirs an emotional response based on the viewer's perception.

Beliefs

We all believe in something....if you don't believe in something then you believe in nothing, which is the belief in something! Recently my 9 year old daughter decided to become a vegetarian. Our family is a long line of meat eaters and we enjoy all types of food. She came to me and stated "Daddy, what would you think if I didn't eat meat?" My response, "It is up to you, but why have you decided to be a vegetarian?" Her response, "I realize its killing animals when you eat meat and I don't believe in harming God's creatures".

Fair enough....well thought out and a valid reason - FOR HER! Her identical twin sister stated "well that may work for you, but I am still going to eat meat," and thus two sets of beliefs, neither "wrong," just different views, personalities and perspectives.

People gravitate towards the different. What works for some may or may not work for others. The same holds true in reasons for and against working for a specific company. If they do not hold to your values and beliefs, you would be miserable.

I was on a social media project for a high end, luxury leather company and was working with a young lady to build their social platforms; she was a strict vegetarian working on a leather brand. I asked her if this presented a personal dilemma due to her beliefs and personal stance on leather as it is produced from cowhide. She was fine to work on the project, and added a real value and perspective since we were sensitive not to brag about our leather-making process to her NOR in any of our campaigns. Our sensitivity to her personal beliefs helped us to connect differently to consumers and not associate the leathers with cow skins!

Know what you believe and stand for, use social media to gauge a company's belief for or against your core values. It will save you a lot of headache in the future.

Desires

In my late teens between university studies, I would work odd jobs to earn money. One summer I earned more than enough cash for books, classes and beer! I had an "extra" $800 just burning a hole in my pocket. The decision was made as I strolled through the mall and found the perfect gold necklace i.e. "gold chain". I purchased the most obscene accessory that no man should ever own! Fast-forward 15 years, 1 wife and 4 kids later to a yard sale which fetched a whopping $25 for my "investment". Talk about desires gone wrong (not to mention terrible branding)!

Think about that one thing you want more than anything in the world! Those few things that you love and must possess! Desires drive attraction and they change constantly! Remember those jeans you HAD to have or the jacket you HAD to own! Where is it six months later, one year later, five years later? Moments of desires drive decisions, much like my gold chain!

Your personal brand should leave people wanting more! I have a friend that is the diva of social media. She was building her brand long before anyone thought about personal branding.

She is one of the most connected women on LinkedIn and is a highly sought after speaker. She recently changed jobs and took an entirely new career path leaving the world of recruiting and going to the social communications world. A mutual friend pointed out that the new employer "must have paid a lot of money to get her".

It is rare to completely change career direction AND receive a pay increase! Obviously we don't know her income level. We do know that she created a desired brand. Her brand screamed "knowledgeable" "creative", "innovative" and "expensive". This all started with a desire to grow professionally and investing personally!

Your social strategy must create a desire in people, a desire to know you and want to work with you. Only through social media can this be accomplished in a short period of time. As I am writing this, I have just wrapped upped a paid speaking engagement, have three pending requests to lead lectures on social media and recruitment, completed an interview for a major media outlet and scheduled a photo shoot with the media outlet for their upcoming story on social recruiting! All of this started in 2005 when I started building my brand on a fairly new platform called LinkedIn.

Use social media to invoke a desire among employers to hire you for your expertise, no matter how long you have been an "expert"!

Senses

Taste, smell, hearing, seeing and touch make up our five senses. Brands have the ability to entice all senses, but your personal brand will appeal to the visual and audio senses (appealing to the other senses may land someone in hot water for activity unbecoming). What do you want people to SEE and what should they HEAR?

Every social platform requests the same basic information; so here are a few things to prepare for;

- Have a professional headshot common to all your platforms
- Create a bio that provide personal and professional information in a short, concise format
- Utilize custom URL endings with your name or the same variation of your name
- Be active in social media, this is the equivalent of hearing!

Many years ago I had a friend that was interested in dating a waitress at a restaurant we would frequent. As regulars we began an informal relationship, but after some time and many visits, friendships and trust began to develop. The good news is they began to date and had a long term relationship. Although this did not end in marriage the dating period was a positive experience for both.

Social media is the same; people get to know you through a platform where you build trust and social relationships. You later become a trusted asset and viewed as a subject matter expert. This has paid in personal dividends. After five years of building my brand, I am paid for speaking engagements and sought after as a resource on the topics of social media and recruiting.

Personality

Every brand has a personality! Nike's "Just Do It" is synonymous with athletics and doing what it takes to get things done! When you see the silver Apple you think of a high end product and the best in consumer electronics! You must communicate your personality through your social branding. Most social networks are not dating sites where you make up a personality and be what you want to be....you must hold true to who you are and display your true personality and not just create a new one!

One particular example of this is an interview I conducted with a lady that had a great fashion blog. It was extremely colorful and all the patterns were spot on! She created quite the social buzz and her brand personality matched her perfectly throughout all platforms she utilized. Funny, witty and smart would be the best way to describe her personality. She interviewed exactly as her footprint led me to believe! We were unable to offer her a role, much to our chagrin, however she did end up joining the flock!

If you are unfamiliar with the Flock, Google "Join the Flock" and watch the recruitment brand video for this awesome and well known social media company!

You must understand your personality: Are you funny? Do you have a dry sense of humor? What are your priorities in life? Does your lifestyle fit a certain mold?

Create your personality around these things and ensure your brand personality is real and not a catfish!

Chapter 2

Social Storytelling

"You're on your own, and you know what you know. And you will be the guy who'll decide where you'll go. Oh the places you'll go." - Dr. Seuss

It is not what the story is; it's how you tell it!

Everyone loves a great story, but there is an art to HOW you tell the story. Someone you grew up with was/is a great story teller, perhaps a grandparent, a crazy uncle or some guy in your home town. Stories take time to evolve, there is meaning and passion behind telling it and it is typically first-hand experience and very personal to the teller. Which one of these companies would you want to work for?

Scenario 1:

You should work for our company because we have 100 years of excellence. We are ranked in the Top 100 companies in America and our average tenure is 30+ years with the company. Check out our webpage www.boringbragpagethatnoonereallybelieves.com

Scenario 2:

Do you know anyone 100 years old? Neither do we, but our company was established in 1914 and has survived the Great Depression, Recession and everything in-between. Not to brag, but we have always been considered a Top 100 company to work for - just ask our employees who have stayed with us for longer than you have been alive! Feel free to interact with them and get the real scoop on our Facebook or Twitter page. Read their confidential reviews on www.glassdoor.com

Both of these versions basically provide the same information about a company, however version two invites you to seek out data from employees versus being "pushed" information from a marketing arm of the company. Now, let's do the same thing with your cover letter to a prospective employer.

Cover Letter #1:

To whom it may concern;

I am writing this letter to express my desire to be a member of your company. I have always admired your organization as a top company in your field. I have a degree in _____ with a ____ GPA and feel I would make a great addition to the team.

I am a member of (A GROUP I PUT ON MY RESUME BUT WAS NEVER ACTIVE) and even held a leadership role (which is crap because my roommate started the group). This experience combined with my can do attitude and academic achievements make me an ideal candidate for this role....

BLAH, BLAH, BLAH........ AND MORE BLAH!!!!

Cover Letter #2

Mr/Mrs Jones

I understand you are seeking a _____. I would love the opportunity to discuss this position. I have an updated resume at (include a link to your on-line resume) or you can view my LinkedIn profile.

After speaking with a few of your employee's on-line and reading employee reviews, I know your organization is a great match. I will offer you hard work, willing hands and a creative mind.

If you decide to review my background, please don't hesitate to contact me with any questions via email or phone (I accept all text messages as well).

In closing, I have included a link to a short video that explains why I can help _____company succeed!

Best regards

NAME

What is the difference in the two versions? The first one is vague on detail, vague on passion and gives lots of "facts" that companies see through. The second paints a picture and take you into the mind of the storyteller. Potential employers want to feel a connection to the storyteller, your brand! You must create a desire for them to dig around more about you. Your opening story line should take them down the trail you have designed.

I connect everything to my blog! My blog is where I retain a video about myself and a copy of my updated resume. If I applied for a job, I would send my resume, but also provide a link to my blog. Guess what? My resume contains links to my blog and LinkedIn profile!

Create a looped trail that brings everyone back to your brand. The more they dig the more they will find the brand crumb trail that you left!

The New Resume: Digital Storytelling

Many years ago students were told to find a high quality paper to ensure their resume stood out. People would send resume via 1st class mail (do you even know what that is?), FEDEX overnight (total waste of $6) and other "creative" ways to get their resume in front of the hiring manager while many times it went straight to the trash can.

Today's job market is a Roman coliseum of competition; lions, tigers, gladiators, and in the end only one winner. In this battle you win by telling the best story! Think of the one of the greatest storytellers of all time; Dr. Seuss! When you were too young to read, your parents read "Oh the Places You Will Go" and you laughed at the funny names and words. Once you had the ability to read, most likely you enjoyed the story and how it entertained, yet seemed all over the place. You may have received this book upon graduating high school or even college, because now you realize it was a book that focused on an entertaining and honest way about the real world and the challenges you would face.

How do you create a story that brings your accomplishments to life in the mind of the reader? How do you tell the story of the multitude of learning opportunities for which you can draw a well of knowledge? How do you stir the emotions of the viewer to understand the aspects of your life and create a desire for them to pay you a sum of money to add value to their organization? How do you do this in a way that stands out and is short and to the point? Answer: It's not just one or two pages of sentences and bullet points.

A digital story unfolds over the course of time; you just need to be the guide, oh the places you will go!

LinkedIn

I simply cannot stress enough the importance of LinkedIn. It is the equivalent of Facebook for professionals and simply the best tool for networking with recruiters and hiring managers. In 2012 while working for a young, startup organization we hired 109 people globally. The organization was a dream job; dogs are allowed in the office, flip flops are worn every day, Friday beer runs, and of course, working with a global brand that had celebrity endorsements and hands-on learning opportunities. **50% of people hired were found through LinkedIn!**

The header, which is the top portion of LinkedIn, is the first impression you will make on people viewing your profile. This is the place with your picture and provides the opportunity for you to add a "tag line" with approximately 150 characters/spaces allowed. Below are recommended example for students:

LinkedIn Heading Example 1:

Marketing major at The University of Awesome with a passion for digital and successful internships to back it up!

LinkedIn Heading Example 2:

Engineering nerd at The University of Awesome with a pocket protector full of knowledge and a GPA that my mom brags about.

LinkedIn Heading Example 3:

Soon to be graduate of The University of Awesome with a major in English and a strong GPA seeking a role as a _____.

These examples are fun, creative and catch the attention of the person viewing them. A more straight laced heading (example 3) is acceptable, just remember to show YOUR personality and keep in line with YOUR brand. Don't get too carried away and let's not resurrect Mr. sleepwhenyourdead69 just because you "are not currently looking!"

Another important first impression portion of LinkedIn is the summary section which allows you to write a brief synopsis about yourself. Starting with a "life quote" can be good, others may think it is cheesy....I say make it about YOU! Also be sure to summarize your history. Obviously depending on your age and station in life, this may be short, but certainly you can include your capabilities, dreams and goals in this section. Below is the example of my LinkedIn summary:

Do or Do Not, there is NO try!" - Yoda

I have built and led 3 highly successful global talent attraction & branding teams (Case-Mate, Panasonic - Mobile and DataPath). Currently I am the Director of Global Talent Acquisition for Case-Mate, a fashion, mobile accessory company that is growing globally!

My passion is talent attraction and recruitment branding. I specialize in storytelling via digital media and creating new/digital media campaigns and recruitment brands.

The consummate family man, I enjoy spending time with my wife and 4 children and am active in my church and community. I am the author of "Social T-Rex ™" | The Blog, best defined as a creative, fun and informative blog regarding my passion for talent attraction and new/digital media.

Feel free to contact me with any questions via the following: alex@alexputman.com

Lastly: ROLL TIDE!!!

This profile summary provides a glimpse into my work life, personal life, my passions, contact information and personality. Anyone reading my profile has made a decision; they like me or don't like me. You have to decide if you care about "they like me" or "they don't like me", but always stay true to your brand!

Experience Section

Treat this section as your "resume", the place where you discuss your previous work experience, internships, co-op's and/or jobs held in school. You can add videos to this section, request referrals (HIGHLY RECOMMENDED), and attach honors and awards.   Once complete you have the option to export your profile as a PDF and utilize as your traditional resume. LinkedIn serves a much higher purpose than just another social profile; it is the one stop place for updating your professional profile.

Networking with LinkedIn

Once you have the profile complete, begin a campaign to connect with every professional you meet and know.

- Family you babysat for – connect!

- Professor or teacher from school – connect!
- Your parents or their co-workers with whom you know on some level – connect!
- Close friends and their parents – connect!

In the world of networking and social media it is who you know and who you are connected to. I found a dream job via LinkedIn and only two people knew about the opening, I just happened to be connected to one of them and I did not know her personally, only professionally!

In 2012, my LinkedIn profile was ranked as one of the top 1% viewed. I have a 100% complete profile and have been a member since 2005 with over 5,800 1st level connections. If you want an example of the correct way to build profiles check out: www.linkedin.com/in/alexputman Your blueprint for a successful on-line presence includes profiles, engagement and being interesting and relevant. The "basics" for your story includes a strong LinkedIn profile, an open enough Facebook profile as to not appear to be hiding something and an unlocked Twitter account where you actually follow recruiters and engage them on a regular basis.

LinkedIn will be the most important social platform you utilize, spend lots of time perfecting your profile!

Video

I am a HUGE fan of video! If a picture is worth one thousand words, then video is worth one million! There has been a surge in video resumes, video interviewing and anything related to video. Whenever I hire interns or co-ops into a creative or marketing program, I require they submit a video in 3 minutes or less and tell me why my organization should hire them.

Most platforms including YouTube and Vimeo allow for you to set up a profile with an "About You" sections. Create a separate channel to host your "about you" video(s). Keep it at two minutes or less and make it interesting. Take the following steps:

Storyboarding

Design the layout of the story just as you would for writing a paper. When I initially designed my introductory video on my blog, the idea was to take four decades of my life and communicate my passions, interests and desires through words and pictures. I have been amazed at how well received this has been and landed a job based on this video (view "My Story" on http://www.youtube.com/socialtrex).

Once I had the theme of "four decades," I pulled pictures, wrote text and determined how the decades would be laid out; early years, college years, professional years and a touch of personal. The general order of a storyboard is;

1. Your Life to present
2. Where you are from
3. How you chose the school you attend or will attend
4. Work history (CO-OP's or Internship) using logos
5. Visual of passions/hobbies

Of course I utilized music (which was non-offensive, did not use profanity nor refer to any portions of the human body and what the artist wanted to do to these areas). The last piece of music was $12 download from Audio Jungle, http://audiojungle.net . This is a great location for royalty free music that is unique and adds a special touch to video.

Putting it all Together

Once the storyboard was complete, I utilized Microsoft's Movie Maker (free) and started building. My experience with videography was limited as was my budget, but I desired something cool that would make me stand out! Most people use a Mac (my next computer) where the video capabilities are tremendous! Just play around until you get the video you desire.

WARNING: I once had someone attempt to copy my video format in a quick and short cut effort. This made the person look lazy and incompetent; my advice is to do it right or have someone else do it for you! The downside to a crappy video is the same as turning in crappy work.

Blog

I started my blog in May 2010 and received less than 10 visitors in my first month (and those were most likely family members or me checking from work)! Do you have a subject or passion that you ramble on to your friends or classmates about? Why not put this passion in written form or better yet high yielding SEO form! People are apprehensive about starting a blog for several reasons. The most common excuses are that they have nothing to say or the fear that no one would be interested in what they have to say.

Blogs showcase someone's knowledge of a subject; my blog is about social media and recruiting! Creating a blog is simple with free tools such as Blogger (Google product) or WordPress. Update 2-3 times per month minimum and, in no time, you will be surprised how often your blog or name appears in Google search. A few tips;

1. Create a blog name that is unique, not difficult to spell.
2. Utilize your real name for blogging as to appear in search.
3. Great writers are avid readers, pick up books on your subject and read them.
4. Blog as you speak, people who read blogs are not impressed by your vocabulary, it's more about the communication.
5. Create an "About Me" section that highlights you and host your resume and social links (the ones you want people to find)

Blogs help control the content you place on the internet. Content is king/queen, so blog often, but never force it!

Chapter 3

Social Strategy

"The way to get started is to quit talking and begin doing." - Walt Disney

Life seems to be one big outline, so how is it we never really think about outlining a strategy for our social footprint. I would recommend for everyone to sit down and create an outline for your social future. This chapter is dedicated to that outline. I have utilized this plan for my personal strategy but also for the strategy of many clients including authors, small business owners, non-profits and luxury retail brands! The five basic components of a strategy include:

1. Mission
2. Target Audience
3. Goals
4. Benchmarks
5. Challenges

Design Your Social Strategy

Below is a basic outline for your social strategy. This chapter will outline unique strategies for LinkedIn, Facebook, Twitter, Videos and Blogs with best practice and interaction using the five basic components. Your overall strategy should look something like the following;

Mission

To build and develop a social network of friends, who will become ambassadors of my brand and assist in my personal and eventual professional growth!

Target Audience

My target audience or user group/network will include;

- Supportive friends
- Family
- Teachers/Professors
- Past & present co-workers

Goals

- Develop relationships through social media
- Build a professional network to assist in my future
- Add value to my connections and be viewed as a valued resource of information
- Increase my footprint online
- Engage potential employers

Benchmarks

- My peers on social media are doing _____ *(View company pages and see what interactions are taking place)*

Challenges

- Positive engagement
- Creating value added conversations
- Keeping it clean and real

Now you have a good overall strategy, but let's break down the strategy for several key platforms!

LinkedIn

If you take one thing from this book, if you implement only one strategy, be sure it is LinkedIn! What appears to be "an old persons tool" very well may be, but you need to engage the old people on their turf and LinkedIn is the home field!

Mission

Develop professional, business related networks for my brand that will create conversation and grow footprint.

Target Audience

- Employers/Companies where I see myself working
- Hiring managers at organizations
- Recruiters within companies
- Professors and people in the business community

Goals

- Create and update my profile on a quarterly basis
- Connect to two new professionals per week
- Request references from all employers during co-op's, internships or other employment
- Follow companies that I would love as a future employer
- Copy the habits of peers that have used successfully

Benchmarks

- Receive _____ new connections
- Receive ____ references quarterly
- Receive ____ views on my profile

Challenges

- Maintain network along with all other activities
- Standing out without much professional experience

It took me three to four years to develop a LinkedIn network and it continues to grow with me year after year! Start early and build it organically! I have found jobs personally and hired many people through this platform. Many of these hires would never have been made, without the tool and this personal network! Bottom line, get on it today and be active!

Facebook

Your strategy for this platform is not about public or private; it is about how to engage companies on one of the largest social networks available. In 2013, one billion people were members of Facebook! It may be a dying tool among 16-24 year olds, however when you are trying to engage 30+ year olds, they will maintain a presence on Facebook.

Mission

Engage and interact with companies and brands in an informal setting professionally.

Target Audience

- Employers/Companies conducting in-depth research about me
- Friends that tag me in videos and photos

Goals

- Create and update my public profiles content
- Understand the privacy rule changes to ensure my profile does not harm me
- Engage and interact with companies on a personal level.
- Learn about opportunities that may not be publicly posted

Benchmarks

- Interact with ____ companies per month (long before a formal interview)
- Build ____ new professional relationships per quarter

Challenges

- Controlling what other post and tag you in
- Keeping up with the ever changing privacy formats
- Learning how to interact with companies in this forum (this book should have assisted in this area).

I predict that Facebook will become less of a personal tool and more of a business engagement tool. My prediction: It will replace the traditional phone book!

Twitter

140 characters to express a thought or idea and engage a group of people of which 70% of the content goes unread! The challenge with Twitter, it's a "tribe" product not a mass marketing tool! Your strategy should revolve around personalization of content and how to engage a group of people, not number of followers and tweets!

Mission

Constantly engage and follow networkers, recruiters and companies to keep up with the latest news and events.

Target Audience

- Employers/Companies
- Recruiters

Goals

- Provide relevant content that is consumed by a small tribe
- Interact with brands and people on a regular basis

- Follow hashtags of professional events and seminars to understand their business
- Cross pollinate my blog and video strategies to another forum

Benchmarks

- Number of retweets receive on content
- Grow follower to _____
- _____ number of engaged followers
- Retweet _____ post per week

Challenges

- Tweeting on a regular basis
- Creating engaging content of interest to people

One of the early mistakes I made with Twitter was attempting to grow a large following because it looked better to have 20,000 followers than 586. Truth be told, I would prefer to engage 586 people than have 20,000 porn stars, wannabe rappers and fake profiles that spam up my feed.

Never, ever use the so called seeding programs to grow your following. The concept is that you provide your handle and then follow people; in return people will follow you. Yes, I fell for this one and spent the better part of a few days deleting the followers that added NO value! Organic growth and time are the keys to having a healthy "Twibe".

Video

Video will be the toughest strategy to incorporate into your portfolio. Content takes a creative eye and shooting videos is only a smartphone away. The overall goal to video is using a tool that many candidates / jobseekers don't, but using it in a way that makes sense.

Mission

Provide engaging content that highlights my abilities and visually sets me apart from other people.

Target Audience

- Employers/Companies
- Recruiters

Goals

- Create VLOG (video blogging) content regarding my subject matter expertise.
- Build a video showcase of my talents and capabilities.

Benchmarks

- Number of views
- Channel subscribers

Challenges

- Regularity of videos
- Creating engaging content

I suggest creating a series of webisodes highlighting key achievements. For students, possibly chronicling the beginning and end of each semester or freshman through senior year or perhaps a video diary of your internships/co-op? The real challenge is getting the right content to highlight on a channel to accompany your digital story.

Keep in mind, the majority of channels catalog your viewing history; ensure that what you are watching does not reflect in poor judgment or taste. I once noticed a candidate that viewed several derogatory channels aimed at minorities (this person even went on to suggest these channels as "humor") – IDIOT! Needless to say, I did not find the humor nor did they find a job with my assistance!

Blog

One of my personal favorite tools is a blog. I have actually hired several people that I found due to their blog! This platform allows a glimpse into the creativity through words. During the creation phase, ensure that you are writing as a subject matter expert on a single or multi-related subject. This is a great way to showcase your knowledge.

Mission

Create regular content on my passion subject that engages readers and creates a high SEO return for my brand!

Target Audience

- People specific to my subject matter
- Future employers in the industry of interest

Goals

- Receive high SEO return on my subject and name (more difficult if you have a common name i.e. Jane Smith)
- Create a blog calendar and sticking to it
- Learn more about my subject as I write
- Engage other blogs and industry experts
- Cross pollinate videos into vlogs

Benchmarks

- Readership
- Subscribers

Challenges

- Calendar out your blog content
- Creating engaging content of interest to people

The fashion industry is one example of creating a buzz around expertise with perhaps little to no experience. In one role as the Director of Social Engagement for a luxury brand, I developed a blogger outreach program to contact some of the more trafficked fashion blogs and pitch our product lines. Many were in their 20's age wise but had attracted enough attention that we were willing to promote our brands through them!

The real key here is building a blog that promotes what your brand is about. Never attempt to discuss a topic you are uneducated or disinterested in, it will show!

Strategy Conclusion

We have covered a lot of material regarding the strategy behind your social footprint. Several may find it as overkill; however those serious about anything will have a plan and stick to it! Your strategy may and should be slightly different than presented above. Remember it's personal to you! This book can provide tips and tools but in the end, it is up to you!

Chapter 4

Using Social Media to Find a Job

"Never quit. It is the easiest cop-out in the world. Set a goal and don't quit until you attain it. When you do attain it, set another goal, and don't quit until you reach it. Never quit." – Paul "Bear" Bryant

Corporate recruiters and hiring managers find talent via on-line networks and communities. Over the past several years my #1 source of hires has been through social media; primarily LinkedIn. Finding a job through social media is much more than simply having a profile on a social network. It is about engaging employers and a key component of your digital story!

LinkedIn

The #1 thing I tell any person, from an entry level student with no experience to a 30 year veteran, is you must have a complete LinkedIn profile! This is an important part of your story as it allows for video uploads, profile picture, organization information etc... You have an option to create a PDF resume from your profile, so why not just create everything in one place!

I have a complete profile and LinkedIn ranks profile strength! The stronger the profile the more likely you are to show up in searches. The next few images are examples from my profile. Although not actively seeking a job my brand is active. People see my profile which is increasing my personal brand awareness! On the next page are LinkedIn stats regarding views of my profile.

PROFILE STRENGTH

All-Star

Views Appearances in Search

Total Views **1,662**

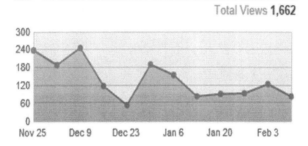

WHO'S VIEWED YOUR PROFILE

5 Your profile has been viewed by 5 people in the past 1 day.

48 You have shown up in search results 48 times in the past 1 day.

Simply having a profile is not enough! Join and participate in groups, questions & answers sections and update your profile status regularly. Following companies is a great idea, since you will get information outside of the static website and companies put a large emphasis on their LinkedIn presence!

Lastly, request recommendations from managers (past and present), peers, professors, internships and anyone else willing to provide one. Recruiters will look at this section over conducting a reference check! However recruiters are not fooled easily, having your sorority sister or fraternity brother recommend you is like asking your mother what type of person you are.....they already know the answer mom will give!

The key to success with LinkedIn is being an active user and engaging others. When I utilized LinkedIn in my search I literally spent three days staring at my stream and sending an email to every recruiter in my network as they appeared in stream. The email was a canned message stating that I was in the market and looking for consulting or full-time gigs! Within two weeks I was working at a great organization with everything I was looking for in a job! This would have been impossible without having a BIG network and an active voice.

Twitter

The best use of Twitter for candidates is to follow recruiters/hiring managers/companies. Believe me, most recruiters love themselves and many see themselves as a rock star with full access to hiring decision and large egos (not me, I am awesome and humble ☺). But what is the best way to interact with these "tweeters"? I suggest the following:

- Retweeting their tweets; this shows that you have an interest. Not the retweets about breakfast or their favorite team winning....retweet the stuff that matters, the jobs they post, links to business related tips, etc...
- Follow people and companies and speak to them on Twitter. Direct messaging is ok, but put it out there, you never know who will see it.
- Share information with and from others in your network with no hope of gaining something in return.

- Follow people that follow you!
- Register with directories such as http://www.Twellow.com (free)
- Follow conversations via the hashtags (#) on twitter such as #jobs or events!

The next picture depicts a quick search on the #jobs hashtag.

In this example, I did a quick search for #jobs and highlight three major companies hiring and posting jobs via Twitter! Twitter is more than a short messaging tool, if used properly it actually serves a purpose in your job search! I can attribute at least five hires from 2012 as a direct use of twitter….the indirect impact could be higher!

Facebook

People think of Facebook at a way to keep in touch with friends, but there are thousands of companies with business pages. Recruiters see Facebook as an area with over a billion users which means there are many potential candidates! Corporate applicant systems are now building software around Facebook to attract and disperse jobs. Facebook has even created a job network of sorts with BranchOut.

Here is a snapshot of my company page, notice how the jobs tab is on the front;

When you open the jobs tab, you will find a listing of jobs that you can apply for directly. My page is powered by a free tool that automatically imports jobs and allows people to apply easily.

eCommerce Channel Manager Atlanta, GA	Jan. 4, 2013, 4:39 p.m. Share · Apply
eCommerce Merchandising Manager Atlanta, GA	Jan. 4, 2013, 4:36 p.m. Share · Apply

You should be interacting with companies on Facebook! As an employer, I have held many conversations through a fan page or corporate site. During a search for a Customer Service Representative, we had 500 applicants apply in 24 hours. It is impossible to go through this many candidates, so companies will start at the beginning and work their way through until they find three or four viable candidates. If you are applicant number 276 and we find the three to four interviewees by number 112, you are out of luck!

In this scenario, three people reached out via Facebook and I responded to all three; none of which were in my original four! They moved through the process, but had they not connected via the company page, they would have entered into the black hole of resumes!

A few tips when interacting with companies;

- Keep the interaction positive, even if you are rejected for the job; engage the company in a positive way.
- Always go to company pages that you may want to work for and "Like" their page, it does not hurt.
- Recruiters are nosey by nature, adjust your privacy settings and only allow for your basic information to be viewed (profile picture, email address, contact information, etc...).

- Remember your cover profile pictures are ALWAYS public; be careful what you share as cover art!!

It is not enough to "like" the page; you need to interact with company, like their postings, ask questions and/or make comments regarding their product or service. Lastly, don't forget about the job tabs! This is a great place to learn more about their openings and apply through a separate platform.

Blog

Build it and they will come! Not really, but if you build it, write excellent content, promote it, drive traffic to it through other platforms, then they will come! A blog is the one medium that you control everything, the look, feel, URL, content and just about everything imaginable. You decide the format whether it is video or photo driven and all the other cool features.

My blog is searchable, promotes the brand, and leads you back to my Facebook and Twitter pages.

Social T-Rex™ | *The Blog!*

HOME   ABOUT SOCIAL T-REX ▾   ENGAGEMENTS & EVENTS   MEET ALEX ▾   MEET ANASTASIA ▾   CONTACT   COOL JOBS!

From a recruiter perspective, conducting a Google search on key words and turning up a blog is easy. Most recruiters find marketing and creative talent through this function. The more you post on your subject matter expertise the more likely you are to be found!

User Engagement Sites

There are several career sites that have taken the social approach. Sites such as Indeed.com and Glassdoor.com provide opportunities for employees to post reviews, discuss companies openly and view insider data via video and photos about the company. Job sites have traditionally been less social until the last several years. Most of these sites include a company blog, where they flex their job search expertise and offer information and insider scoop!

Chapter 5

The Future of Recruiting

*"**Imagination is more important than knowledge**"* – Albert Einstein

Every time a new social platform comes out, the #1 question that recruiters ask, "How can I use this in recruiting?" Facebook has one billion people and was designed for friends to connect and keep in touch, yet every company has a career page and most recruiters are active participants. LinkedIn started as a business network; now there are 200 million users and about 5% are recruiters. But what if you knew the next recruiting trend? Here are a few of my predictions:

Google Glass

Imagine this scenario; you're standing in a crowded room and notice a stranger wearing clear glasses, perhaps the glasses appear a little bulky or out of place for the event, but you pay it no mind. This stranger keeps staring as if they are reading you like a newspaper....because this will be a reality, an augmented reality!

Google Glass will eventually use augmented reality, which is a live, direct or indirect, view of a physical, real-world environment whose elements are augmented by computer-generated sensory input such as sound, video, graphics or GPS data. I have been discussing and presenting on this for several years and the reality is coming towards the end of 2013. Remember how in the opening of this book we discussed your brand and how you should be aware of whom you are on-line. When I started writing this book, Google Glass was a far cry from reality, upon release of this book it will be a much anticipated reality and once you have bought this book, it will be improved upon!

My prediction: the stranger in the room, staring you down will actually be able to read your on-line history, scanning you and seeing everything Google has to offer. What about when you interview and someone is wearing the same glasses? Interviewing and dating will never be the same!

Mobile

Mobile is already here; however the use of mobile recruiting will grow exponentially over the next decade. Worldwide mobile phone adoption is around four billion, with a whopping twenty-five percent of those users owning a smartphone! By 2014, smartphone use will take over desktop/laptop use. In the United States, Americans spend 2.7 hours per day socializing on their mobile phone!

Most companies are preparing by optimizing their sites for mobile users including career pages. Recruitment brand managers are holding seminars and conferences based solely on the growth of mobile! One key example is the way PepsioCo created a mobile app "Possibilities" solely for people, especially potential candidates, to interact with their recruiting team.

At a glance, PepsiCo is focused on connecting and engaging, beyond just a job search. Some of the functionality of the "Possibilities" app includes:

- o PepsiCo Twitter feed
- o Content for why, the people and the brands
- o FAQ's

- Ways to connect with Recruiters.

- Scanning their brands with a stickybits partnership

- The Feeds from the lineup of PepsiCo blogs

- PepsiCo YouTube

- Geo-location job search functionality

They have incorporated every aspect of the social experience into a mobile application. PepsiCo is large enough to pull this off, but as mobile apps become easier to create and smartphone adoption continues to grow, look for more companies to embrace this or a similar technology that may not exist at the moment!

Talent Communities

What is a Talent Community? It is an environment consisting of people who can share ideas for the purpose of career networking or social recruiting of candidates

The idea of a talent community is similar to a tribe or village. Companies want to identify candidates from pools of people and include them in a group they engage beyond a "one time, we have a job please apply." A talent community is a select group that has been identified as high potential. Perhaps you interview and turn down a role or the role is closed or you just are not ready to make a move; recruiters have always kept a "black book" and now the talent community concept provides them an online ability to engage this black book of talent consistently and well past the "I have a job" phase!

Let's get into the mind of the employer. Why would they take time and spend money to build this type of network? Why utilize and invest resources into a company like Ascendify

http://www.ascendify.com to build this type of community?
The top reasons include:

- Makes it easy to reach qualified candidates

- Candidates are consistently engaged to their business

- Less dependence on traditional job boards

- Less money spent on job advertisements

- Increased interaction with potential candidates

- Provide insight and clarity of your organization

- Better quality of applicants to job openings

- Creates a talent pipeline for future job openings

- Attracts passive candidates

So why would you want to be a part of these communities?
Think of it as a career investment! Over the course of your
career you will change jobs multiple times, why not be in
control of these changes.

When you become part of a corporate talent community, they
will provide additional value beyond "we have a job opening"
such as;

- Send you company updates or an e-newsletter not open
  to the general public

- Providing "VIP" information on new job openings and
  internship programs

- Create contests and opportunities for you to engage
  beyond the resume

- Provide inside information via blog posts

○ Communicate and connect via social media.

Look for employers to become more exclusive in their hiring and candidate selection. They will utilize all the latest social tools and seek candidates from non-traditional methods. This is why building your brand and presenting your image online is beyond critical! It will make the difference in your career!

Chapter 6

How to Impress Employers

"I told them my system was based on the "ant plan," that I'd gotten the idea watching a colony of ants in Africa during the war. A whole bunch of ants working toward a common goal."
– Paul "Bear" Bryant

What does a termite hill and architecture have in common?

The Eastgate Centre is a shopping centre and office block in central Harare, Zimbabwe whose architect is Mick Pearce. When Mr. Pearce was commissioned for this work he was given a set of interesting instructions for a luxury building; find a way to control the temperature without a HVAC system! Now in many regions of the world this may not be a difficult task, however in Zimbabwe, you have a desert and the temperatures of the desert range from extreme cold in the evening to extreme heat during the day!

He was able to design the Centre without HVAC which saves the building $4 million dollars on an annual basis while maintaining a consistent and comfortable temperature all day! How? He studied the architecture of a termite mound!

The indigenous termites built mounds which uses tunnels to cool control temperature at an even 82 degrees. Mick Pearce designed the building with the same series of tunnels and flow as to create a temperature controlled system for a large building in the middle of the desert!

Innovate and creativity took over, which is exactly how you must think and prepare! Ask yourself the question; how can I use the tools and technology today to stand out as a candidate for employment?

Apply Innovation

This is one of the best examples of creativity ever! This "resume" was sent from a student seeking an internship within the creative field. My understanding is he got the internship! Use your mobile device and click below to see his innovative resume.

Scan with QR App

There are many other ways to apply innovation. Perhaps it is not as extreme as above, but what can you do that no one else or very few people are doing. Controlling your social brand is an important piece to all this. Anytime a new social network becomes available (which seems like every day) I think, how I can use this to attract talent? You should be thinking, how do I use this to stand out to an employer?

Another example of creativity can be found at http://phildub.com. This person built his resume as an Amazon purchase complete with social links, ratings and contact information!

Personally I built an "about me" section on my blog complete with video and resume download! I did land a job because of this page with a creative organization who was seeking nontraditional styles in human resources.

Notice the short video introduction, the call to action "Do you have 1 minute", "….watch 4 decades of my life…."

How to Impress an Employer

Scan the QR code in this section for a quick (3 minute) video that I use in all my jobseeker presentations

Scan with QR App

Stand Out as a Candidate

Albert Einstein said it best *"Imagination is more important than knowledge"*.

Having interviewed thousands of people over my career there are many that stand out; but it may be 1% or less! I have categorized the memorable ones for the wrong reasons into the following categories

- "Out all night at a bar, smoking cigarettes and not prepared"
- "Is this a strip club or Hooters interview, since that's how I dressed"
- "Call the police, because I must be on a wanted poster due to my dumbass comments"
- "Pull your boots up, because this crap is getting deep"
- "I'm so awesome, just listen to what I have to say about myself"

Let's focus on how to stand out in the right ways.

Communication

A friend of mine is the head of HR for an international electronics company with commercials and products all over the world! He posted a message sent to him by a candidate that he did not have a job for;

Subject: *New Suit $300, New shoes $50, New haircut $20, being able to interview with your company...well that would be priceless!*

When asked, "did you give him a shot" the response was "I don't have anything he fits, but it made me want to open a position!"

Was this subject line original "no", was it memorable "yes!"

Presentation

You will either present yourself in the eyes of an interviewer as a "yes" or a "no", there is no in-between! Within the first seven seconds (yes that is correct, SEVEN seconds) anyone you meet with has already formed an opinion of you!

I was interviewing several people for a role in my department. My requirements were basic; I wanted a person with capability versus someone with exact past experience. Following the traditional path, I interviewed people from the industry, with the right degrees and backgrounds.

Working in a cool/hip fashion environment, things were less than traditional. In walks a young lady, she had the right degree, sounded great on the phone and by all accounts had the job in the bag! Upon entering the interview one thing was clear; she was trying too hard. It appeared as if she watched the company brand video and decided to uncomfortably change her entire wardrobe! She literally wore a dress that was about the length of a t-shirt and, I can honestly say, she had on white unmentionables! It was a difficult interview and for the first time in my career I was speechless. Afterwards, we did provide her with constructive feedback; wear pants or shorts with your t-shirt!

Weeks later, I had the joy of meeting Anastasia! She came from a slightly different background but instantly I could tell she was extremely intelligent, well-spoken and had an air of confidence! Her outfit was not prudish, not business, but very well put together. She entered with a firm handshake and direct eye contact. She was able to connect her experiences to what I required in the role! Hired, promoted and to this day, one of the best hires of my career.

But what did she do so differently? She did not try "too hard", she was herself! I later learned that she toiled for hours on how to dress for the interview. We always instructed people, "come as yourself and no business attire required", which sometimes made it more difficult than going with your interview suit! Present who you are and be who you are and it will work out much better in the long run!

Confidence

You walk in the room with your best suit on, you make direct eye contact, smile, say hello and reach out to shake the hand of the interviewer and miss! Your handshake is weak, or you slip or just miss it much like the passing of a baton during a relay race. How do you recover? Simple: you state "Hey, sorry I missed that handshake, let me try that again!

Opportunities to exude confidence occur at all stages of the interview process. Employers want a confident (not arrogant) employee, someone that can affect the department and role! I remember my worst example of confidence. I interviewed a young man during a career fair. He was a shy engineering type, so my expectations were geared towards GPA and engineering courses versus his confidence. However when he approached me his hands were almost dripping wet with sweat! He was so nervous that in the 10 minutes we chatted he literally appeared to have jumped out of the shower, he was perspiring profusely and it was all due to nerves (extreme lack of confidence). He shuffled about and did not make eye contact.

I have thought about this young man often, wondering if it were a medical condition or simply nerves. I will never know. However his lack of confidence cost him the opportunity to interview further on this particular day. What should he have done? How could he overcome this issue if in fact it were not nerves and perhaps a medical condition? Simple; OWN IT! My advice to him today would be, if it was in fact something out of his control, "explain this issue up front no matter how embarrassing it may seem." We live in a pretty understanding world and most employers will not be judgmental of these types of issues, if you take the time to explain it!

However on the complete opposite end of the spectrum, I interviewed a student who came into the interview, kicked his feet up and spent the first few minutes telling me how he had a job secured with one of the world's largest and most prestigious internet companies. He asked me how we could compete (he also went on to describe the salary and perks). My response to this overly confident young man was simple; I have no interest in competing with them for his talents and sorry he wasted his time and took the spot of someone else that may have wanted to interview with us.

Be confident in your abilities and actions, but remember to not be a jackass!

Likeability

Whenever people sit down to meet with candidates they typically walk away with one of the following thoughts;

1. I really liked that person, unfortunately they are not a fit due to _____
2. I did not like that person because they were _____
3. I really liked that person and glad they are a fit, let's take the next step!

As an employer even if I don't have the ability to hire you today, if I like you than I am more willing to assist in your networking. Perhaps I have a friend or colleague that can assist? Perhaps another opening becomes available and I will think of you!

Tickets for Sale

We were interviewing Mechanical Engineering students out of one of the top schools in the nation. This particular school was performing very well in basketball that season just as March Madness was approaching. A critical game was scheduled against a conference rival and the #1 team in the nation was scheduled. Students were camping out for the chance at tickets!

My interview day was set during this week and one promising student did not show up for the interview during his allotted time (which he scheduled and was responsible for cancelling). When he no-showed, I removed him from my list of consideration. As the day was closing the student pops in (5 hours late) and asks if I have time to meet with him. I always attempt to provide the benefit of the doubt, so I said I would give him time if he could answer one question, "Why did you skip your interview and not call to cancel or reschedule?"

I am sure you see what is coming; he stated that he was in line for tickets to the big game and was excited that he received fruits for his labors. I told him that I totally understood and would have done the same thing, except I would have cancelled the interview. He could have even given me the real reason and that would have been 100% cool! Yet he wasted everyone's time.

Over the years this particular student reached out to our organization regarding employment. We had a great program for students and the organization is regarded as a great place to work. The hiring manager and I both recalled him by name and never met with him.

What we did not like was his attitude and irresponsible behavior....if he had called and cancelled because he was getting tickets, we most likely would have worked with him and he would have flourished!

Rejection with a Happy Ending

Another occasion found us meeting with an excellent entry level software development student. She had a wonderful personality, great GPA and was a leader inside and outside of school! We offered her the job and she turned us down, rejected like the class nerd by the homecoming queen!

This was the first rejection by a student for our company, students WANTED to work for us. Another time and different company, we were actually rejected by the reigning Miss University of Georgia Queen! She took another role where she would make less money and have career progression opportunities.

Alas, both these scenarios have a happy ending. Both of the ladies rejected us and within 2-3 weeks called back to say they felt as if they made a mistake and would love to be reconsidered! We liked them so much from a personal and professional side that they were both hired and worked five plus years with the respective organizations!

Bottom line, if you have skills and are likeable, you will not have a problem getting a job offer (again)!

Five Opportunities to Stand Out

There are five opportunities for a candidate to stand out in the interview process. These stages are all touch points between the candidate and potential employer. Be sure you are aware of these points and stand out at each stage. The stages are outlined below;

Submittal

You want to stand out to the right person. How did you apply for a job? Did you follow up with a hiring manager or contact? I always recommend finding a hiring manager, the decision-maker for the role. Depending on the size of the company, you may go to the top! I have worked in small and mid-size companies and received resumes from the CEO-not knowing if he/she knew the person-but if the CEO sends it, the person is getting a call!

You can find this information many ways, however I recommend LinkedIn! It is the best company research tool imaginable. You could also conduct a Google search or just call into the company, explain that you are a student (really a student in this case) and trying to get your foot in the door. If the person answering the phone says "no", ask for their email address because you want to thank them for their time. Guess what? The person you are trying to reach will have the same email style i.e.

FIRST NAME.LAST NAME@COMPANY.COM. Now you are in and cooking with peanut oil!!

Discovery

Discovery is when the company is getting to know you. First impressions will always be visual. Be aware of how you are applying? Did you follow up? Are you speaking with the decision-maker? I always recommend an on-line version of your resume. Beware these sites come and go quickly! LinkedIn is still the best place to create your online resume, however a few good (and free) sites include;

http://about.me

http://www.careerigniter.com

http://www.resumebuilderonline.org

You should always link your social profiles including any video. A few common items to be aware of include customizable addresses and easy to share social media sites.

Interview

Now you have the interview....DON'T SCREW IT UP! You need to make sure you do the following;

- Arrive 15 minutes early!
- Sharply dressed but don't overdo it!
- Be aware of body language and eye contact...and cleavage.
- Be prepared to back up everything on your resume, the big question in their mind is "how do I know this is not BS."
- Listen and engage in two-way conversation.
- Sit up straight, lean slightly forward and hands on the table (if no table put them on your legs or whatever, just don't appear nervous or uncomfortable).
- Don't be defensive.
- Never bad mouth anyone, especially a past employer (you learned something from them, it can't be all bad)!
- Be who you are, don't compare yourself to others.

Post Interview

The interview is over, you have left and now what? Don't leave until you understand the next steps and actions required by you. Remember to stay professional and send thank you emails! Don't be a stalker but do follow up!

Some great follow up ideas:

- Hand written thank you notes (no one does it anymore) – if it's a creative company/position, be sure to get creative!

- Email thank you note (few people send any type of thank you).
- Follow up with additional questions which are a sign of thought and interest in the role.
- Email follow up with reasons you are a fit for the job/company.
- Provide an article or newsworthy tidbit about the company or industry.

Decision

The desire to hire will come down to five things, most are within your control.

Factors Companies Consider After the Interview

Many things impact a hiring decision; however once you have interviewed, the employer will be mulling over five key points when making their decision; skills, impact, culture, attitude and reputation.

Skills

My personal belief is that job descriptions are a thing of the past, however many traditional organizations do not see it this way. My rule of thumb is to hire someone that has at least 75% of the skills required with the ability to learn the rest! Talent assessment is extremely subjective in most fields excluding medical, engineering, accounting and other specialized areas.

Employers deploy a variety of tactics to determine knowledge match; pre-assessment testing, problem-solving, and the list could go on. Be sure that you have a solid understanding of the required and desired abilities as these are two completely different things. When discussing an opening with a hiring manager I always request the two or three "must have or don't show me" capabilities and then communicate these directly to candidate. This is out of your control, you either have them or you don't....however the desired skills is completely different. You need to convince people that you can learn these or at minimum transfer some of your current talents.

Impact

Employers now, more than ever, want to know what impact this person will have on their business. In order to communicate your abilities in this area, you must provide examples of your impact. Perhaps you are sixteen years old and seeking that first job ever. Communicate volunteer opportunities and how you made something better than when you started. Perhaps you have a role within your school; sports, band, drama etc.... You should be able to communicate more than "I was on/in the team/club", you must paint the picture of someone that impacts change!

When someone has minimum experience, a great way to gain knowledge is through volunteering. Honestly, I was never much of a volunteer in college; however fast-forward to my interest in social media. I volunteered for the local Atlanta chapter of the Society of Human Resource Management and became the Vice President of Social Media, which led to the Executive Vice President of Marketing, which created the opportunity for me to develop social media plans, which I then used for my companies luxury brand line, and in the end led to my idea for this book!

Through volunteering, I turned a passion into a career. Many will ask if doing all that work in a volunteer capacity paid off....YES in experience and eventually YES in monetary form!

Culture

All companies are different, some require you to wear a full suit with tie, others are shorts and flip flops. Many are business causal with the khaki pants and polo shirts allowing for jean Fridays! But culture is more than the clothing; some companies are full court press politics, while others are no nonsense, and get the work done, while many require one hundred twenty-seven pages of documentation and approval to order ink pens.

The question will always arise; does this candidate fit into our culture? I wish I could say it is different than high school, but it is not. Even in the entrepreneurial startups, with the dogs and skateboards, a person's "cultural fit" will always be an issue.

My personality is one of get it done; build it, innovate something, and keep moving or move on! I was interviewing with a large, financial services company that had a desire to be the "Google of financial services!" I'm thinking, "Score!!!"

The first stage of the day began with a required Wonderlic test while awaiting the results in a holding area. Once the results were graded and I "passed", I moved to stage two or, as I like to refer, "Stooge Two". I was escorted down a long hallway with no real signs of life by one man wearing an ominous suit and into a room being greeted by two new suites. I quickly realized the lack of a cultural fit or glimmer of hope for a "Google wannabe" After a grueling two hour interview I was asked if I had any questions; I stated "Yes, in fact I have only two".

Question 1: "What is the most innovative thing the HR department has done this year?"

Response (*after a 5 minute pause and puzzled looks all around*): "Well, we just installed a new payroll system and everyone is getting paid on time….."

Question 2: "Did you guys wear the suits just for me?"

Response *(in a very serious, matter of fact tone):* "Well no, this is everyday attire, is that a problem?"

Actually, yes, yes it was!

Attitude

In the story above, my attitude was most likely evaluated as "somewhat negative." Having much insight into the process, I detected early that this was not a culture for me. I actually broke out my "transgender work story," knowing full well that all though true, may not be the best example of dealing with a sticky situation! I did not want the job!

If you want the job, have the right attitude. When discussing past employers, no matter how bad they suck or how terrible the job, keep a positive attitude. The interview day can be a long and grueling test, but be prepared to stay positive!

Questions often revolve around situations; the goal is to understand how you handled these situations. Your past actions predict your future behaviors and companies will pick apart every answer. Be prepared to provide situational analysis of your past in short, concise bits.

Formula for storytelling

Start with the situation, describe the problem, provide the solution and close with how it affected the company! Now for my work place transgender story…. (You didn't think I would drop that bomb and not follow-up, did you?)

I was working for a government contractor and we had often placed civilians with past military experience in hostile war zones to provide service to our products. Imagine being in the middle of Iraq during war time in closed, cramped military quarters.

We made an offer to a man around the age of sixty. He was a great match for the job technically; however upon acceptance of the offer, he requested a special accommodation. This is not unusual in the human resources world, as many employees require accommodations for a variety of reasons. This person was requesting a separate bathroom due to his surgical changes were only 50% complete.

This is obviously not a situation one comes across every day. In this case, an accommodation was out of our control. We were unable to provide an accommodation (and not legally obligated too) since the work zone was on a military base (not our work site) on the other side of the world. We were able to explain this to the candidate and document why we were unable to make the accommodation.

The situation: Potential employee requesting a special accommodation.

The problem: We had no control over the accommodations and this was a rare incidence given the nature of the work.

The solution: We researched special accommodation and attempted to offer other options for the role outside of deploying to the war zone.

The Effect on the company: No one was sued, no bad press was leaked and we were able to handle in a professional manner with no legal casualties to the organization!

Maintain a positive and "can do, will do, have done, if can't will learn" attitude and you will be fine on this part of the evaluation! If you don't know how to do it, that's what Google is for!

Reputation

There are two types of reputations; a good one or a bad one.

Online is no different, you either have a good brand or a bad brand (having no brand can be considered a bad thing as well). As one of the factors in hiring, this may be the most important. In all my years of recruiting, one stat as held true; employee referrals account for between 35% - 50% of all hires!

Outside of an employee referral, Google serves as the end all of people search. As you can imagine, background companies stay busy and with the change of the social landscape, more people information is available to background check companies. TalentWise is a background check company that can actually scrub your social networks and look for many variables regarding your online reputation.

Have you posted a joke that contained derogatory or negative comments regarding the race or sexual orientation of someone else? Have you been tagged in a post that appears in your stream regarding illegal activities, if only as a "joke"? This could come back to bite you since this company is searching for these variables and reporting them to clients.

Remember, build your brand early and ensure a good reputation! You never know what will come back in a future employer's search results!

Chapter 7

What to Expect in an Interview

"If you do not expect the unexpected you will not find it, for it is not to be reached by search or trail." -
Heraclitus

You have done everything outlined, you have built your social brand, created a digital story OR perhaps you are just starting this journey. Either path, you have an interview looming. Let's discuss this stage and best practices for nailing the interview!

Phone/Video Interview

The point of the phone/video interview is to quickly assess the talent pool for a particular role and make a decision on the next step. I have conducted thousands of these and had qualified individuals completely screw up this important part of the process. What is the best way to make a great 1st impression when the interview is not in person? How do you NAIL IT?

Never be caught unprepared. If you receive an unexpected call for a phone interview, the first question from the caller will be "is now a good time to chat". If you are unprepared or need to gather your thoughts, simply request a more convenient time (within a few hours or at the convenience of the caller) to conduct the phone/video interview. This gives you time to prepare the following:

- A set of good questions (see interview questions section).
- Immediate research on the company/person calling (LinkedIn, Facebook etc...).

- Relax and gather your thoughts.

Always prepare like it is an in-person interview. Anytime I have conducted a phone/video interview and see/hear shuffling of paper, or keyboard strokes, it is a huge negative (I may assume you are cheating with Google, attempting to find the answers to my questions)! If it helps, put on your interview suit and conduct the phone/video interview in full interview mode.

Interview in a quiet place with NO distractions! No matter who/what the distraction is; drunk roommate, hot neighbor stopping by or the dog barking, you must secure a NO DISTRACTIONS area!

Land line or great WI-FI connection is essential! Don't conduct a phone/video interview while driving down the road or walking to class! Chances are good you will drop off (no matter your provider) and there will be interference and you will perform poorly.

Initiate request for in-person interview at the end of the call. When the company says "can you come in sometime next week?" the answer is "YES!" Know your schedule before-hand, and schedule quickly!

Talk with confidence. Confidence will come across in your voice, in your answers. Confidence is a direct reflection of your preparation and practice, do both of these relentlessly.

Follow these simple NAIL IT principles and you will have an advantage over 75% of other candidates. I am constantly amazed at the number of people who blow the phone interview because they do not take it as a serious part of the process.

Don't be that person.

Do's and Don'ts of an Interview

You can never be reminded too often of what to do and not do during an interview. Just when I think everyone understands the concept of interviewing, I meet with someone that blows that theory out of the water. I don't consider myself the Taylor Lautner of the interview world; however I have been flirted with, shown extraordinary amounts of cleavage, experienced the dragon effect (terrible breath), and seen someone sweating so bad it appeared that he just stepped out of the shower! So please take the 15 minutes required to read through these basics of interviewing!

Display Your Personality

No matter the job, the level of the role or the basic skills required your personality will be observed and measured into the following key areas:

Attitude   Appearance   Confidence   Approachability Professionalism

Attitude

- Thou shalt not lie!

- Voice inflections and nervousness always give you away!

- Show the enthusiasm and passion for your field, major and/or accomplishments! A person with no passion for their accomplishment will not have passion in their new role.

- Express your passion for the type of work you want to do, this displays an interest in the subject matter.

- Don't be nervous; this is easy to say, but you must find a way to relax (minus drugs and alcohol, as this will lead to a different set of issues). Besides, you must already have a good chance since you got the interview!

Appearance

- First impressions take less than seven seconds!

- Maintain positive body language.

- Be on the lookout for certain gestures that communicate negative messages, such as poor eye contact, hurried nodding or crossing your arms.

- Posture, body language, and manners are still at the top of the list.

- Differentiate yourself from others; find a way to make an immediate impact (this does not mean wear a crazy tie) but perhaps a really definitive suit/shoes (again not crazy, just cool).

- **PRIVATIZE your social networks.**

- Basic presentation issues:

    o No cologne/perfume/powder odor.

    o No ornate jewelry.

    o No chewing gum/mints/cough drop.

    o Turn off (not to vibrate) your cell phone.

    o Don't bring water bottle to interview.

    o Have a professional email (nothing like partytillidrop@url.com).

    o Bring a notebook/portfolio and pen; show basic initiative by appearing prepared.

- Image is a paramount consideration for any interview.

    o   I would recommend ensuring no visible piercing along with the usual, nice hair, clean teeth, etc….

Confidence

- Be a listener and engage in a two-way conversation.

- Make direct eye contact.

- Sit up straight, lean slightly forward with hands on table.

- Firm handshake, if you miss the shake, ok to say "hey, let's try that again."

- Never take a defensive stance on a question (honest answers).

- Don't complain about workloads, hours worked, your boss etc…

- Do not speak negatively about anyone.

- DO NOT compare yourself to other people, be your own person.

Approachability

- Allow the person interviewing to LIKE you and visualize you in the role.

- Smile; for five plus seconds when you enter a room and when you say "nice to meet you."

- Make eye contact for two extra seconds when being introduced (and saying goodbye) to someone new. One-one-thousand…two-one-thousand…

- Develop an unforgettable answer to a few common questions.

- Sit with toes pointed AT the speaker (pointing signifies resistance – subtle but true).

- **Discover the CPI, or Common Point of Interest**, between you and any new friend as soon as possible. Ask creative, unique, interesting, thought-provoking and challenging questions like, "Can you describe the best day you had at work last year?

- Keep your hands away from your nose or mouth while talking; it is a display of dishonesty and discourteous.

Professionalism

- Arrive 15 minutes early.

- Make sure you understand the employer's next step in the hiring process; know when and from whom you should expect to hear next.

- Know what action you are expected to take next and DO IT!

- Back everything up by solid detailed scenarios or experience.

- Personal thank you's and not just an email.

- LinkedIn profiles need to match up with their current resume.

Experience

Candidate's first reaction to receiving an interview typically assert the following thought process "Do I have the past experiences, right internships, correct pedigree the company is seeking"? However, employers are not only looking at past experience as a direct match, but also in terms of have you done "things" that can translate into my required skill sets. I have hired many people that did not have the "right" experience, but did have the capabilities, let's chat about Brooke.....

The Wedding Planner

Several years ago, I was hiring a talent acquisition assistant and interviewed 20+ people but could not find the organizational skills and personality desired. I then interviewed a young lady, right out of school with a great personality. She had me in the first 7 seconds (personality, confidence, solid handshake)! Then we discussed her upcoming wedding and HOW she was planning for her nuptial bliss. I invited her in for an interview and requested she bring her wedding planner (folder) that she poured months into! It was phenomenal; the book was extremely organized and had detailed plans. See I did not need a person with x or y job experience, I needed a set of skills!

I hired her on the spot and 6 years later she was managing a Human Resources group for a major global organization!

I would have loved to hire a person that had supported the talent acquisition function; however, I was really hiring a skill set. Her talents did not lie in past experience, but how she communicated her personal experiences into my key accountabilities.

Now, let's break Experience down into three groups;

Jobs   Initiative   Education

Jobs

- Know what the company is hiring for and be prepared to address how/why you fit or do not fit the role.

- When discussing your skills, be honest about what you know and don't know; most importantly know how your skills transfer into what the company needs.

- Have a prepared list of references from previous employers (co-op's, internships, professors and managers) that will address your skills (e.g. she is highly organized because ____)

- Describe what you like most about previous positions and also be prepared to describe what you like least (don't speak poorly of previous employers, but know your likes and dislikes)

- Know your resume; you should never need to "refer" to it during the interview (you wrote it and did it, right?)

- Be prepared to discuss your career goals and your plans to achieve these goals.

- Be realistic; many skills transfer, however I am a marketing major involved in Talent Acquisition, Talent Management and Human Resources – I AM NOT AN ENGINEER, some skills will not transfer.

- Volunteer work can translate into actual work experience, don't forget to include in your profiles and during your interviews.

Initiative

- When interviewing bring tangible information to the interview (portfolio, tablet with presentation of achievements, etc...) this WILL set you apart.

- Ask for contact information (a business card or email address).

- You may also want to load the CardMunch app from LinkedIn, simply take a picture of the card; it will search LinkedIn for the person and then send an invite!

- Discuss projects or work assignments where you identified an issue, suggested a solution then implemented your suggestions.

- Define what motivates you professionally and personally (if you don't already know, then soul search and figure it out).

- The definition of initiative is: an introductory act or step; leading action! Companies should not have to walk you through basic parts of the process (completed application, prepared reference lists, having an id, clean background checks – if this is a problem, address up front!)

Education

- Clearly show all education, continuous learning and training; show how you are growing intellectually as well as professionally.

- Education, continuous learning and training should match your goals; highlight how they match your goals (even if your degree is not in line with your field, find a connection).

- Address GPA concerns directly; explain low GPA's and never shy away from the discussion. If your GPA is low, discuss your GPA in your major (if higher), or discuss how you financed your own school (if you did). Bottom-line, be honest and address these concerns up front.

Bottom Line: you may have more experience than you give yourself credit for...but be realistic in your search (for a job and your skills).

Relationship

The term "relationship" can be used in many ways, but when people are interviewing someone, they try to find a common / instant connection. The question you should answer is "how do I immediately connect with the interviewer?" This does not mean walking into the interview and showing off your cleavage! Most employers have already searched for you on Google, LinkedIn and other networks in an attempt to connect with you on one of these three levels;

1. Knowledge (what do we know about each other)

2. Experiences (relating "real world" experience to each other)

3. Business acumen (understanding the mutual business insights of each other)

Each level ended with "each other", because the interview involves two people. Each person is meeting with a purpose in mind and the end result is the formation of a relationship.

Knowledge

- This goes without saying, but really research the company you are interviewing with. You should know what they do, company size, locations, a little about their operational methodology, basically as much as you can!

- Research (LinkedIn, Google, Facebook, etc....) the people conducting the interviews, if possible. In a few pages you will read the "Bagel Girl" story. Turns out we were both alumni of The University of Alabama and I actually knew her brother in school (small world and instant connection).

- Know about the role for which your being interviewed:

    o regular tasks

    o typical goals

    o key accountabilities

    o expected deliverables (week 1, month 1, 6 months, 1 year)

    o Be able to demonstrate how you can perform these initiatives and provide clear examples from your past.

Past actions predict future behavior!

Real World Experience

- Relate your professional experiences to the goals and objectives of the company. What can you do for them versus what they can do for me!

- Chances are the hiring manager has performed your role, the more you know about them, the better you can relate your experiences to some of their past experiences.

- Discuss your career transitions and how you handled them; i.e. when you went from an individual contributor to manager, when you left college and went to work for the 1st time.

Business Acumen

- All employers want to know that you understand how business in general works AND that you have an understanding of their business

- - Metrics driven resume = metrics driven employee

  - See the big picture, it is about the company not you (communicate this)

- Be able to talk to your interviewer about recent company results, products, projects, mergers, acquisitions and share performance; this will show them that you are truly interested in their business as opposed to just getting a job somewhere.

- When interviewing, you should be able to discuss their company's recent business events with the hiring manager, but be ready to give your opinion, in case they ask!

- Answer questions with specifics and numbers ("Data entry made up 60% of my summer internship" or "I input 2500 client files into our database")

Bagel Girl

Some time ago, I interviewed a young lady for a sales role. I was slightly apprehensive, because her resume was spotty (several jobs with little tenure). She was an alumnus of my university and we later discovered that her older brother and I knew each other, having travelled to New Orleans together for what I will refer to as "field study" for the sake of this book and the written proof within.

Within the first few minutes of the phone interview, I knew she had knowledge of our industry, she related her experiences to me on a personal level (both from the same state, same school etc...). Many of our professional experiences were similar and she clearly expressed this connection. She interviewed a few days later and I was blown away by how much she knew about me professionally, our company and the position we were hiring. She got the job and is doing wonderful!

Note: It did not hurt that she agreed to interview at 7:00 a.m and brought us bagels; her reason for the bagels, she knew we would be hungry and not eaten breakfast that early!

What did she do that was so right? For starters, she brought food and utilized my social footprint to discover things about me that most people would not know (however a quick Google search would reveal). She nailed the three keys above.

Communication

Interviewers will judge your communication on more than just verbal (how well you translate your thoughts), they will also evaluate you on:

1.   Written (your resume, application, paperwork etc…)

2.   Body Language (what are you really thinking vs what you say)

3.   Questions & Answers (how well thought out, relevancy to the interview – i.e. not canned)

4.   Ability to Listen (indicates how you will take direction)

Written

- All paperwork (resume, application, forms) must be well written, neat, clean and complete; this will reflect your work style to the employer.

- Writers are readers, how many blogs, books, articles have you read about this topic?

- Size matters; when you write something go back and try to make it shorter with the same or more impact

- Read your resume / thank you notes out loud: Make sure they flow and sound memorable.

Verbal

- Leave a lasting impression; make sure the interviewer knows what they need to know about you.

- Don't start your conversation with

    - "I was just going to say…"

    - "I'm not sure if I'm right, but…"

    - "I don't know if…"

    - "This is probably a stupid question…"

- Use self-disclosure openings as conversation starters, they ease communication apprehension.

- Be ready to offer insight into you and appeal to the inherent helpful nature of other people. Examples include:

    - This is my first interview (if it is)

    - I am really excited to learn more about your company (this will open them up to ask, "Well, what do you know"), then tell them!

Body Language

- Interviewing is like dating, be engaged in the conversation and the person!

- Connect with the interviewer, they should feel as if you are an old friend and you're catching up!

- Research positive body language for interviews, a few tips include;

  - Smile when entering the room.

  - Firm handshake (if you miss simply state "hey, let's try that again), this shows confidence.

  - DO NOT fold your arms.

  - MEN: Never, ever, ever CROSS YOUR LEGS, it may be taken as a negative.

  - DO NOT put your elbows on the table.

  - DO NOT clench your fist (indicates anger).

  - Sit down after the interviewer.

Questions & Answers

- Always ask GOOD questions about the company, the person(s) conducting the interview.

- Start with an introduction, followed by a question like: "What else can I tell you about myself?"

- Ask questions throughout, be conversational, but precise.

- End with a good question: "Was there anything you were looking for that we haven't discussed?"

Ability to Listen

- Don't talk yourself out of a job, relax, always be confident and professional.

- Pay attention to verbal and non-verbal cues.

- Prepare responses to "standard" questions with 30 – 120 second responses that drive home a point

- Repeat back key points from the interview and address them in your response.

- Above all LISTEN!!!

Investment Worthy

Employers want to know that when they hire you there will be a return on their investment. It may sound one-sided, but remember you also want a return (training, experience, contacts, network etc...) So how do you communicate your value?

Every interview I ask myself, "Is this person worth the investment?" When I boil it down, I really interview on two key items: leadership potential and goal achievers.

Leadership

- You must communicate to employers that you have the ability to lead in some capacity!

- Discuss your involvement as a leader, no matter the roles (no role is too small);

  o Sorority/fraternity

  o Charities

  o Intramural sports

  o Church activities

  o Clubs/organizations

  o Projects

- Leadership and management are two completely different things, be sure you understand and distinguish the differences

    o Leadership: to go before or with to show the way, to conduct by holding and guiding, to influence or induce, to guide in direction, course, action, opinion, etc...

    o Management: The act, manner, or practice of supervision.

- Discuss why people want to follow you (in team settings or when you led a project).

- How do you influence outcomes that are in the best interest of employers?

Goals

- Discuss your short and long-term goals; be ready to explain your **plan** of achievement.

    o If your goal is management (a common response), then discuss the steps you are taking; i.e. reading books (give title of book), taking classes, volunteering to manage projects etc...

- Clearly communicate your professional and personal goals.

    o Professional first; discuss your previous career path and key milestones.

    o Discuss why you chose previous employers or positions that tied into your professional road map.

- - o Have a professional road map!

- Achievements

  - o Discuss recent goals you have achieved and how you achieved.

  - o Don't be shy, you are in an interview to sell yourself, but don't be arrogant.

General Interview Questions and Answers

Aristotle said it best, *"We are what we repeatedly do. Excellence, then, is not an act, but a habit."* Once you are in the interview process, you can expect a series of open-ended questions. Below are a few general, sample questions. I have taken the liberty to provide a framework for the answers hiring managers are seeking.

- Tell me about yourself?

  - o Focus on personal and professional values.

  - o Why you chose your career path.

  - o Highlight experiences (life, career, education etc...) you are proud of

- What is your greatest accomplishment?

  - o Choose an example that was helpful to an employer or project.

  - o Discuss *how* you achieved the success, not just that you achieved success.

- What is your greatest strength?

  - o Focus on top 3 (1 may not be enough, however more than 3 may give a negative impression.

- o Leadership skills.

- o Team-building skills.

- o Organizational skills.

- What is your weakness (improvement area)?

  - o DO NOT SAY: I tend to expect others to work as hard as I do," or "I'm a bit of a perfectionist" or "I work too hard"

  - o State your true improvement areas and how you are working or have worked on them.

  - o Employers want to know that you are aware of your shortcomings and willing to do what it takes to improve

- How do you handle stressful information?

  - o Tell how you use time management, problem-solving or decision-making skills to reduce stress.

  - o It is fine to discuss your work-out regiment

  - o Don't make a "poor taste joke" such as "I kick the dog"...yes someone really told me this, they did not get the job.

- What is the toughest problem you've had to face, and how did you overcome it?

  - o Tell a story here, 2 minutes should be enough time (discuss projects that were off schedule, job search in 2009 etc...).

- o Answer from a professional standpoint (one example may be overcoming the transition from manager to individual contributor, etc...).

- o Do not discuss personal issues such as bad relationships, divorce, or how you partied too hard the prior night! TMI...

- o Personal problems that are acceptable include; putting yourself through school, overcoming an obstacle to reach a personal goal etc...

- Why do you want this position?

  - o Here's where your research about the company will help you stand out among the other candidates.

  - o Discuss the pros of the job and how your skills match.

  - o Openly discuss any shortcomings you may have and present how you will overcome – instead of being the person "that has never made a mistake."

- Why are you the best person for this job?

  - o Emphasize several reasons why you should be hired (skills match, behavioral match, company cultural match).

  - o DO NOT provide "canned" answers such as:

    - "Due to my extensive experience in (insert job function)."

    - "I'm a fast learner."

o   Provide detailed answers such as:

- Due to my extensive experience in (insert title) and skills in (key items they are seeking from the job interview).

- Provide an example of times you had to learn something quickly, how you came up to speed and the final results.

Questions to Ask Yourself after the Interview

You have done everything outlined in this book! Your brand is phenomenal, your social presence is impeccable and you have sailed through the interview process. You have several companies interested and need to make some decisions. Do not base your thoughts around "what the job will pay!" Ask yourself these 12 questions to evaluate the best fit!

1. Who did you speak with and how much time did you spend with each person?

   o   Longer is better, hopefully your interviews went the full schedule or longer, this is a strong indicator of company interest.

2. How did you get along with each interviewer?

   o   This is your potential boss and/or peers. Your first impression may be your best impression of them.

3. What questions did they ask and did you have any problems answering them?

   o   Evaluate the type of questions and your level of comfort with the questions and interview styles.

- o This could be your home for a while, be sure you are comfortable with the expectations.

4. Were you able to give full details regarding your experience? How well did you communicate your thoughts? If a question threw you off and you now have an answer, add it to your follow up!

5. What information did you learn about the company that you did not already know?

    - o The internet and static web pages are great, but did you learn something about the culture or environment that you could not find on-line?

    - o Was the information positive or negative?

6. What did you like most about the company? Position? People?

    - o Evaluate this closely; this may be the most important question you ask yourself.

7. What are the negatives in your mind about the company? Position? People?

    - o This is a lot like dating; can you live with the negatives of the company?

    - o Yes, they do have them, so if none were identified then you should have more questions.

8. What did you think about the location?

    - o Consider the commute or geography of the company. Be realistic and consider the impact to your personal life.

9. Based on what you know now, if an offer was extended, would you accept it?

    o   (If yes, what is the bottom line base salary) You may even want to take out the dollar figure and decide if this is somewhere you would work regardless of compensation....higher salary will only make a place bearable for so long.

10. (If no) What questions do you need to have answered to accept the position?

    o   Create a list and get them answered, you may be surprised at the clarification to many of them.

11. Are you willing to walk away from all current and pending interviews to accept this position? Why? Why not? The real key is why or why not!

12. Do you want the job?

The next step is to follow up with expression of interest. This should be a handwritten "thank you" note and/or an email/phone call to reiterate interest. You would be surprised how many candidates forget this step and how many companies still put stock into this practice!

Chapter 8

Testimonials

"Do or Do Not, there is NO try!" - Yoda

We have covered a lot throughout this book. You may be asking yourself, does this stuff actually work?" Below are several real life testimonials of people using social media in their job search with success and a few uh-oh moments!

I Hired My Stalker

Over the past several years, my blog has grown quite the following. It is well advertised on all my social networks and was the driving force for writing this book. While working for an uber cool and sexy start-up company, I had an opening for a Customer Service Representative. Within 24 hours we had 500 responses and, to be completely honest, whomever we selected was going to be the luck of the draw!

Suddenly, I received an email via LinkedIn and a new connection request. One day later a new follower to my blog and comments on a recent post. Later I receive and email as follows:

Subject: Do or Do Not, there is no Try - Yoda

Greetings Mr. Putman,

Thank you for connecting with me on LinkedIn. I noticed that quote on your profile and I thought it sounded perfect for me. I have been trying to get in with (Bad Ass Company) for months now and realized it was a "Do or Do Not" situation. I am confident that if I could just meet with you for a moment, I would be a great fit for your organization. I'm sure you are a busy man, but if you could just spare a few moments I would relish the opportunity to meet with you and show you that I could make an excellent addition to (Bad Butt Company).

Thank you for your time and I look forward to hearing from you.

Warm regards,
Keith

He connected the very first line of my LinkedIn profile and made it personal to me. I love Star Wars (nerd alert) and believe in making things happen. This candidate not only got an interview and took the job....I WANTED to hire him! I was rooting for him even though he was visibly nervous in the interview. The 2nd thing he did correctly was have another connection send a recommendation for him as follows:

Subject: Keith

I understand you recently interviewed my dear friend Keith. He is a top notch individual and very hard-working. You cannot go wrong in hiring Keith for your Customer Service role as he has the capabilities and strong desire to work for (Bad Butt Company).

Best regards

LinkedIn Connection

I did not know either person, however by following their digital footprint I knew they had been co-workers and had a professional relationship. To this date, the candidate is still working and thriving at the organization!

Keith and I still joke about how he "stalked" my profile and he introduced himself to my wife at the company party as my "online stalker!" She laughed and said "I am use to it!"

I Got Hired Because of Twitter

Tracking hiring sources is a key measurement to recruiters. We want to know what sources work and which ones are time wastes. Twitter is a commonly overlooked tool, but Lauren may argue that point. At age 22, she was a recent graduate and hoping to find that reputable company who placed a high value on employees.

Her search started with campus recruitment and scouring the campus job boards and email job blasts. She hoped to avoid the job boards because she felt they were impersonal and only led to the "black hole" of job search. Once per week email blasts were viewed as spam!

She decided to move to another source-LinkedIn-where success was found in terms of reputable companies. Previously when she would find a potential job, she would Google the name of the company with "spam" in the search and review Glassdoor.com for insider reviews. She was amazed at the number of pyramid or multilevel type "sales opportunities" existed; however she stayed true to her goal; connect to real people with real jobs!

Remembering her intern days she began to follow the recruiting team from her previous company and found that when the team posted jobs they used the hashtag #iamhiring. She would then search #Atlanta #iamhiring. Within days she found a sales job with the company whom was my employer for four weeks. She immediately applied and became an employee within three weeks!

The job she applied to was not posted on LinkedIn, and at the time the company did not have a designated career site. Her goal with Twitter was to connect to real people, within a real company! Months later she was promoted, and at the time of this writing, is assisting in sales efforts for Canada!

Facebook Mom Returns to Workforce

Dayna was a stay at home mom and decided to return to the workforce after twelve years! She reconnected with an old friend from high school on Facebook via a status update requesting prayer for her decision. Her friend (who was a Human Resource Manager) sent her a direct message offering resume and job search assistance! Within three weeks, Dayna landed a full-time job!

You Are What You Tweet!

In 2009 we worked with a key client and placed a temporary contract employee in an Executive Assistant role. This was a great opportunity for a young person with a Fortune 500 company and most likely would have led to a full time role. People stay at this company an average of 30+ years and one of their Presidents worked his way up from the mailroom! Within the first few hours of employment, the contractor tweeted out "not many of us people in this place" and tagged the company. Several tweets later defined what "us people" meant as the employee (who was African-American) made several comments derogatory to the companies hiring of African-Americans. She was terminated instantly!

She was making derogatory comments in social media and tagging the company within a few hours on the job. The fact is this particular company employees one of the most diverse groups of employees within the metro area, has been awarded numerous times for their diversity efforts and places a high regard on diversity seemed to be missed upon this twitter-happy young lady. The comments showed immaturity, lack of understanding and a negative attitude without having all the facts. This person was terminated by the directive of the 3rd C-level in command. Her negative and inaccurate tweets landed her in the unemployment line and without the hopes of working her way up in an excellent organization.

Breast Regards!

Sarah was a web developer working for a company that struggled to pay her, obviously a large concern for anyone working! She began her search for a new role only to be met with several "bogus companies." She explains "I went on one interview and was led into a dark corridor", after a long interview I was invited back the next day and told to bring walking shoes". Turns out this "job" was a door to door sales role, hardly the call any in-demand web developer expects!

She decided to turn to LinkedIn as a resource to identify legitimate companies versus the inundation of bogus companies with serial killer tendencies. She learned of an opening via Indeed.com and researched the company on LinkedIn. She quickly noticed a 2nd degree connection between her and the recruiter with the opening (me)!

Her immediate action was to research the company and myself. Through Google, she discovered my blog, began to study my writings on interviewing and utilized my advice to her advantage. Her 2nd degree connection made an introduction and then she sent an amazing email through LinkedIn;

Mr. Putman,

I wanted to personally reach out to you and express my interest in the UI Developer position you posted on LinkedIn. I saw we had one 2nd degree connection, Brian, who I spoke with and he said you are a great person to reach out to. I used to work with Brian at XYZ Company and he informed me you have spoken at HR/SHRM events for your company. Brian also mentioned, in your speeches you have talked about how great AWESOME COMPANY is, I am intrigued.

Having always been involved at some level with technology, I've also been aware of the ability it has to create our minds desire. As I started to learn more about myself, I realize I am most interested in website development. I have experience in working with CMS, responsive/parallax sites, HTML, CSS, and am familiar with PHP.

I have the practice of training and supporting new employees, and helped resolve technical issues with some of our clients. When clients are using a CMS, I have sat in and trained them how to use the CMS. Working with a variety of clients has provided me the opportunity to work within teams and cross browser platforms.

Working in a team environment is very important to me because it allows everyone to learn from one another and to create the very best result. I am also an independent and self-directed employee, able to work creatively and analytically in a fast-paced environment.

Going through your blog, Social T-Rex, I enjoyed that you not only provide great information but also make it a fun and insightful read. I especially liked the "Inside the mind of the employer" blog.

I am fun, creative, and always eager to learn new information. Thank you for taking your time to read this and I am looking forward to further discussions with you.

Breast Regards, Sarah

"People who say it cannot be done should not interrupt those who are doing it" - George Bernard Shaw

Three weeks later, Sarah was a full-time employee! She did her research via social media, she branded her message based on days' worth of research, and even ended with a quote because she noticed two quotes in my profile! She name dropped, had the person reach out to me on her behalf, "liked" our LinkedIn and Facebook page (and yes, I noticed her footprint all over our social sites)! This ladies, and gentlemen, is how it is done!

Just case you are wondering, "Breast Regards" was an accidental signature, which was meant to read "Best Regards"! If you really want to grab someone's attention misspell the signature with "Breast regards"!

Conclusion

"If you can dream it, you can do it." - Walt Disney

In 2010 I started a blog, http://www.socialtrex.com as storage for thoughts and ideas regarding social media and recruiting. As time passed, the blog became a company where we provide consulting services to companies and their recruitment departments on engaging and attracting talent to their brands through social strategies including: social networks, video and blogs.

Writing this book is a dream come true as I have always desired to write about something; however I have never been passionate enough about a particular topic to write until the last few years. I hope this book is helpful to jobseekers of all experience levels.

This is a culmination of three years' work and brought together from years of public speaking, topical PowerPoint presentations, volunteer work and sixteen years of serving as a hiring manager and recruiting function of many companies.

A few people think that social media is a fad and will go away (much like the desktop computer). Many years from now these platforms will evolve into much more; perhaps Facebook will serve more as a platform for all social networks, similar to Google search. I am already seeing Twitter versions of performance management tools which even today consist of twelve plus pages of tedious year end reviews.

Social media changed the way I interact with people on a personal and professional level. The key is to remember, people are still people, no matter the generation, the background or their socioeconomic level. If you treat others as you wish to be treated, then the world will be a better place.

Don't be scared of technology, take chances and try to utilize the new tools in your career function and everyday life. Create a video and link it through a QR code and send it out to friends and family! Build a resume on YouTube and campaign companies through their social networks. Sit down and read a book. The key to all this is just do something!

Resources

Below is a list of helpful resources and key influencers in the social recruiting world. These resources will be beneficial during your job search and provide inside information regarding social recruiting and your career growth.

Build a Blog

http://wordpress.com

http://www.blogger.com

https://www.tumblr.com

Career Blogs

http://www.socialtrex.com

http://sixdegreesfromdave.com

http://www.recruiterchicks.com

http://www.blogging4jobs.com

http://www.hrcapitalist.com

http://www.keppiecareers.com

http://TheCynicalGirl.com

http://recruitingunblog.com

http://blog.jimstroud.com

http://www.hellomynameisblog.com

http://www.joegerstandt.com

http://www.talentanarchy.com

http://www.tincup.com

http://fistfuloftalent.com

http://blog.linkedin.com

http://www.monsterthinking.com

http://blog.simplyhired.com

http://www.careerbuilder.com/JobSeeker/Blog

http://www.shrm.org

Job Boards

http://www.monster.com

http://www.careerbuilder.com

http://www.indeed.com

Inside Peek of Companies

http://www.glassdoor.com

http://www.vault.com

Online Resume Builders

http://www.careerigniter.com

http://www.resumebuilderonline.org

People to follow on Twitter

@alexputman

@anastasialevana

@teelajackson

@incblot

@jennifermcclure

@lruettimann

@ewmonster

@billboorman

@JasonLauritsen

@jennydevaughn

@keppie_careers

@kris_dunn

@SHRMSMG

@socialtrex

@havrilla

@ewmonster

@williamtincup

@mattcharney

@davemendoza

@cathymisseldine

@joegerstandt

@marenhogan

@jimstroud

@jackwbruce

@jessica_lee

Definitions

Applicant Tracking System: system used by companies for you to apply to their jobs, typically connected to their career page.

Augmented Reality: is a live, direct or indirect, view of a physical, real-world environment whose elements are augmented by computer-generated sensory input such as sound, video, graphics or GPS data

Awesome: see Alex Putman (now I can say my name is beside awesome in the dictionary)!

Blog: created from two words "web log" it is a forum where you can create content (text, pictures, video etc...) and share content with whomever.

Circles: Circles are clusters of a user's friends on Google+.

Connections: Someone you are "friends" with on LinkedIn, similar to a "friend" on Facebook.

DM or Direct Message: allows you to send a message of 140 characters or less to a person that follows you on Twitter.

Follow Friday: a trend using the hashtag #FF on Twitter each Friday. Users choose usernames and tweet them with #FF as a recommendation for other people on Twitter.

Follower: someone who joins your social community and is interested in reading or sharing your content.

Foursquare: is a social network where people share their locations and connect with others. This network is a great source of deals and discounts at restaurants and retailers.

Google+: Google's social network where friends are called circles and you can conduct hangouts (video chatting).

Google Glass: Go to http://www.google.com/glass/start

Hangout : is a video service on Google+ that allows you to video chat with up to 10 Google+ users are a time,

Hashtag: is a tag on Twitter (the # key) and is a way to mark a message. Example #socialtrex will allow for searching on this topic.

Instagram: is a photo sharing app where you can take pictures and alter them with filters. You can then share to other social networks including Facebook, Tumblr, Flickr, Twitter, Foursquare and even email.

Klout: measures a person's "social influence" by measuring an individual's usage and influence on social networks including Facebook, Foursquare, Twitter (most impact), YouTube, etc. The highest score is 100 and the higher your score the more influence you have.

Like: is an action where users click the "like" button on Facebook to show approval for messages or comments.

LinkedIn: is a business-oriented social networking site or the business equivalent of Facebook.

QR code: Quick Response Code, 2-dimensional bar code with a link embedded. This is retrieved via a QR Reader on a mobile device which is typically downloaded for free.

Retweet: When you share content on Twitter and a follower shares the same content, this is a retweet or RT.

Search engine optimization: is the process of improving the volume or quality of traffic to a website.

Skype: is a free application to video chat with other users.

SlideShare.net: is an online social network for sharing presentations and documents (GREAT resource for research and doing presentations.

Social Media: online communication in the form of media that users send out through social platforms to express themselves.

Social Recruiting: recruiting people via social platforms and networks.

Tweet: a message with 140 characters or less sent to a group of people that follow your account.

Twibe: a group of people that are part of your twitter following and actively participate in your content.

Vlog: video blog.

About the Author

Alex Putman started his career in recruiting after graduating from The University of Alabama with a Bachelors of Science in Marketing and minor in Public Relations. He has been responsible for all aspects of talent acquisition and recruitment for global companies on every continent except Antarctica.

In 2013 he officially founded Social T-Rex, a recruitment and brand marketing agency focused on new media strategies for organizations.

He resides in Atlanta, Georgia with his wife Tifany and four children (Alexis, Kathryn, Gabrielle and Corban). He speaks and consults on new media and recruitment marketing on a regular basis.

See "My Story" by scanning below